Lost at the shopping mall

Story by Annette Smith
Illustrations by Susy Boyer Rigby

Jon and Sally and Dad
went to the shopping mall.

They saw a lot of children.

Dad said,
"We have to go
into this big store now."

"Oh, Dad," said Sally.
"Can I stay here?
I can see a little train
in the window."

"I will look after Sally," said Jon.
"I will not let her go away."

"Sally, stay here with Jon,"
said Dad.

Dad went into the store.

Jon saw his friend.
"Hello," said Jon.

Sally saw one of her friends
by the little merry-go-round.

She ran to see her.

Dad came back
with a shopping bag.
"Where is Sally?" he said to Jon.

"She has gone!" said Jon.
"Where did she go?"

Dad and Jon ran to look for Sally.

Sally came back
to the big store.

She looked for Jon.
He had gone away.

Sally saw Dad and Jon
coming back to the store.

"You went away from me, Sally,"
said Jon.

Sally said,
"You saw your friend.
I went to see my friend."

Jon said to Sally,
"We will stay with Dad, now."

"And I will stay with you,"

said Dad.